HEDY LAMARR

Reimagining Radio

Megan Borgert-Spaniol

Checkerboard
Library

An Imprint of Abdo Publishing
abdopublishing.com

abdopublishing.com

Published by Abdo Publishing, a division of ABDO, PO Box 398166, Minneapolis, Minnesota 55439. Copyright © 2018 by Abdo Consulting Group, Inc. International copyrights reserved in all countries. No part of this book may be reproduced in any form without written permission from the publisher. Checkerboard Library™ is a trademark and logo of Abdo Publishing.

Printed in the United States of America, North Mankato, Minnesota
102017
012018

THIS BOOK CONTAINS
RECYCLED MATERIALS

Design: Emily O'Malley, Mighty Media, Inc.
Production: Mighty Media, Inc.
Editor: Liz Salzmann
Cover Photograph: Alamy
Interior Photographs: Alamy, p. 24; AP Images, pp. 18, 23, 29 (right); Shutterstock, pp. 7, 15, 27, 28 (right), 29 (left); Wikimedia Commons, pp. 5, 9, 11, 13, 17, 21, 28 (left)

Publisher's Cataloging-in-Publication Data
Names: Borgert-Spaniol, Megan, author.
Title: Hedy Lamarr: reimagining radio / by Megan Borgert-Spaniol.
Other titles: Reimagining radio
Description: Minneapolis, Minnesota : Abdo Publishing, 2018. | Series: STEM superstar women |
    Includes online resources and index.
Identifiers: LCCN 2017944049 | ISBN 9781532112829 (lib.bdg.) | ISBN 9781532150548 (ebook)
Subjects: LCSH: Lamarr, Hedy (Hedwig Kiesler), 1913-2000--Juvenile literature. | Spread spectrum
    communications--Juvenile literature. | Motion picture actors and actresses--Juvenile
literature.
Classification: DDC 621.384092 [B]--dc23
LC record available at https://lccn.loc.gov/2017944049

CONTENTS

1

HEDY LAMARR

Austrian-American Hedy Lamarr is most widely remembered as a beautiful movie star of the 1930s and 1940s. But away from the studio, the Hollywood actress was also an active inventor. Lamarr's ideas led to an invention that would change the way the world communicates.

As an actress, Lamarr became famous for her looks. Because of this, she had to work extra hard to be taken seriously. People didn't expect a beauty like her to have the sharp mind of an inventor. But Lamarr never cared about doing what was expected of her.

Lamarr's greatest idea came during **World War II**. She invented a system for guiding underwater **missiles**

"All creative people want to do the unexpected."

–Hedy Lamarr

Hedy Lamarr resented her looks. She famously said, "My face is a mask I cannot remove. I must always live with it. I curse it."

by radio. Lamarr thought her idea could help the United States fight German submarines. But the invention had its greatest effect on the development of wireless communication. Her ideas paved the way for **technologies** such as cell phones and the internet.

2

REBEL WITH A DREAM

Hedwig "Hedy" Eva Maria Kiesler was born on November 9. Historians are unsure whether her birth year was 1913 or 1914. Hedy grew up in Vienna, Austria. Her father, Emil, was a banker. Her mother, Gertrude, was a former professional pianist.

Hedy's father encouraged her to use her imagination. He told her exciting stories and took her on long walks. Emil was also fascinated by **technology**. He was always explaining to Hedy how different machines worked. Meanwhile, Gertrude taught her daughter to appreciate the fine arts. She had Hedy take ballet and piano lessons.

Hedy spent much of her free time playing by herself. She loved to dress up in costumes and act out fairy tales. She dreamed of one day becoming an actress.

In 1929, Hedy's parents sent her to a **finishing school** in Switzerland. Hedy was not happy at the school and tried to run away. After getting caught several times, she was

The city of Vienna is known for its music, art, and theater.

finally successful. She took a train back to Vienna and
convinced her parents to let her stay there. They sent
Hedy to a local school, where she studied art and design.

3

A TASTE OF FAME

Still, Hedy wanted to act more than anything else. She dreamed of moving to the United States to become a Hollywood star. One day in 1930, she snuck into a film studio near her school. Once inside, she asked for a job. She was hired as an assistant that same day. Soon after, she was given a small part in a film.

Hedy finally convinced her parents that acting was her future. They allowed her to leave school in Vienna and pursue her dream. In the fall before her sixteenth birthday, Hedy entered acting school in Berlin, Germany.

In the following years, Hedy grew as an actor. She appeared in several plays and films. Soon, she was widely admired for her beauty and talent on stage and screen. One admirer was named Fritz Mandl. Mandl began sending Hedy flowers after her shows. Hedy married Mandl in August 1933.

Mandl was very wealthy and bought Hedy anything she wanted. But his controlling nature made her feel like one of his possessions too.

Hedy soon learned that by marrying Mandl, she was giving up much of her freedom. He was controlling and jealous. He didn't want Hedy to pursue her acting career. Mandl worked as a **munitions** dealer for several European nations. He only wanted Hedy to make him look good to the people he did business with.

4

ACROSS THE ATLANTIC

Kiesler's life with Mandl had become a prison. She wanted to escape. In 1937, she packed her belongings and went to London, England. Kiesler was free of Mandl and ready to pursue her dream once again.

In London, Kiesler met Louis B. Mayer. Mayer was the head of MGM film studios in Hollywood. He was in England looking for new talent. Mayer offered Kiesler a contract that paid $125 a week. But Kiesler knew she was worth more than that.

Kiesler did not accept Mayer's offer. Instead, she joined him on the ocean liner back to the United States. During the trip, Kiesler impressed Mayer. He agreed to give her more money and a longer contract. In return, Kiesler would learn English and change her last name to Lamarr.

The ocean liner docked in New York City at the end of September. The next day, Kiesler boarded a train for Los Angeles, California. At 22 years old, she was bound

Hedy sold most of her jewels to pay for the trip from England to the United States.

for Hollywood, the capital of the US film industry. Hedy Kiesler was now Hedy Lamarr and her dream was closer than ever.

5

HOLLYWOOD SENSATION

Lamarr's first Hollywood film was shot in 1938. It was called *Algiers*. Lamarr played the starring role of a French tourist in northern Africa. The movie was released that July and Lamarr was an instant sensation. People were stunned by her performance and beauty. She had become the international film star of her dreams.

As her career took off, Lamarr enjoyed being a Hollywood actress. But Hollywood life did not always suit her. She found the parties to be boring and tiring, especially as she was still learning English. Lamarr preferred quiet evenings in the privacy of home.

A LIFE IN LOVE

Lamarr's marriage to Mandl was the first of six marriages. None of them lasted more than a few years. She also had two sons and a daughter.

Lamarr (*right*) starred in *Algiers* with Charles Boyer (*center*) and Sigrid Gurie (*left*).

One of Lamarr's hobbies was inventing. Her studio at home was filled with books and drawing boards for sketching ideas. There, she dreamed up inventions for instant cola drinks and facial tissue disposal. She also put her inventor's mind to use in more serious matters of war.

German **Nazi** forces had taken over Austria in March 1938. Jewish Austrians were being put in **concentration camps** or forced to leave the country. The next year, **World War II** broke out in Europe.

6

WARTIME WEAPON

In the fall of 1940, German forces were bombing London nightly. Many British children were being sent by ocean liner to safety in Canada. On September 17, one of those ocean liners was struck by a German **torpedo**. More than 200 people died in the icy Atlantic waters.

After this tragedy, Lamarr became desperate to help the war effort. She had learned a lot about **munitions** and weapons during her marriage to Mandl. Now, Lamarr tried to think of new weapons to defeat German submarines.

One idea Lamarr thought about was remote-controlled torpedoes. Torpedoes were effective when they worked, but their failure rate was high. These underwater **missiles** often missed their targets, exploded too early, or did not explode at all. Lamarr knew torpedoes would be more successful if there was a way to guide them to their targets. Fortunately, she had recently met somebody who could help make her idea a reality.

Torpedoes were launched from submarines or warships to attack enemy ships. These weapons were especially important in damaging Japan's ships in World War II.

Lamarr first met American **composer** George Antheil at a dinner party in August 1940. Antheil was famous for using **automatic** player pianos in his music. These mechanical pianos were able to make music without a human player. Antheil had the **technical** skills Lamarr was looking for.

7

FREQUENCY HOPPING

Shortly after Lamarr met Antheil, she told him about her **torpedo** idea. Antheil was interested in helping with the invention. Lamarr had just begun shooting a new film. But in her spare time, she and Antheil got to work on her idea.

First, Lamarr needed a way to control a torpedo remotely. The console radio market had recently introduced wireless remote controls for changing radio stations. The remote control communicated with the console radio through a fixed radio **frequency**. Lamarr thought radio frequencies could be similarly used to communicate with and guide a torpedo.

This was not an entirely new concept. Germany had been developing weapons

DID YOU KNOW?

Radio frequencies take the form of waves. High-frequency waves run close together while low-frequency waves are more spread out.

George Antheil was considered a musical genius. His performances caused riots as he traveled Europe in the 1920s.

called glide bombs throughout the 1930s. These winged bombs were guided through the air by radio control.

However, radio control of weapons came with the possibility of interference, or jamming. Enemy forces could easily discover the radio **frequency** being used to guide a weapon. They could then use their own radio signal to interrupt the communication.

Lamarr had to solve the problem of signal jamming in radio-controlled **torpedoes**. She knew a signal was easier

While working on frequency hopping, Lamarr was married to her second husband, Gene Markey.

to find and jam when tuned to a single, fixed **frequency**. But if the signal changed frequencies at **random**, it would be impossible to track.

Lamarr called this random retuning "frequency hopping." Frequency hopping required a radio transmitter

The US government established the National Inventors Council in 1940. American citizens could send the NIC their ideas for inventions that aided national defense. The NIC reviewed ideas and connected inventors to the correct divisions of the military.

on a ship and a radio receiver on a **torpedo**. The two devices had to hop from **frequency** to frequency at the same time.

Lamarr explained her idea to Antheil, who had experience **synchronizing** multiple **automatic** player pianos. Now, he and Lamarr worked together to apply that knowledge to radio frequencies. In December 1940, they submitted their idea to the National Inventors Council (NIC). They wanted the US War Department to know what they were working on.

Lamarr and Antheil's first submission did not include a **mechanism** that would **coordinate** the frequency-hopping. Instead, they had a human operator coordinating the hops by hand. Still, the NIC took immediate interest in the idea. Its leaders asked that Lamarr and Antheil continue to work out the mechanical details of their idea.

8

PIANO-INSPIRED PATENT

Over the next several months, Lamarr and Antheil developed their radio-controlled **torpedo**. They needed to develop a **mechanism** that would **automatically** change the **frequencies** of the signal. They decided to model this mechanism after that of an automatic player piano.

A player piano's mechanism used a **scroll** to instruct the piano to play. Antheil proposed a similar mechanism for his and Lamarr's frequency-hopping signal. The radio transmitter station would have one scroll. The receiving station would have a matching scroll. Holes punched in the scrolls would initiate changes in frequency. The scrolls would be **synchronized** so they changed frequencies at the exact same time.

Lamarr and Antheil worked on a patent for their frequency-hopping system. In the process, they received some help from others. They consulted with an

Player pianos were very popular in the early 1900s. Their popularity declined after people became more interested in the radio and records for playing music.

electrical **engineering** expert at the California Institute of **Technology**.

The two inventors also worked with patent lawyers to apply for their patent. They wanted the terms of their patent to include more than just their proposed **frequency**-hopping system. Lamarr and Antheil also wanted to own the rights for any invented **mechanism** that served the same purpose.

9

FILED FOR LATER

In June 1941, Lamarr and Antheil filed their idea with the US Patent Office. They called it their Secret Communication System. Meanwhile, they were still waiting for an official response from the NIC. Examiners were determining whether the radio-controlled **torpedo** could be of use to the US War Department. By fall, the invention had been passed to the US Navy for consideration.

At that time, **World War II** was getting more serious. Japan had taken sides with Germany. On December 7, 1941, Japan bombed the US naval base in Hawaii. Soon after, the United States officially entered the war.

The US Navy rejected Lamarr and Antheil's invention. It did not want to invest time or money in new torpedo **technology** in the heat of war. The rejection letter also noted that the **frequency**-hopping **mechanism** was too bulky for a standard torpedo.

Apart from her inventions, Lamarr did many activities to help soldiers. She even volunteered at the Hollywood Canteen, a club with food, dancing, and entertainment for soldiers.

Lamarr was always confident in her skills as an inventor. When she was informed about an award she had won, Lamarr replied, "Well, it's about time!"

In late 1942, Lamarr decided to help the war effort in a different way. She began to sell **war bonds** to raise money for the country. Lamarr's fame helped her sell millions of dollars in bonds. In one night alone, she raised $7 million!

Lamarr and Antheil were disappointed. They knew it was possible to make their **mechanism** smaller. They also knew how much their invention could have helped their country's naval forces. But there was little they could do to convince the navy to develop their idea.

The inventors were still waiting to hear back from the US Patent Office. In August 1942, Lamarr and Antheil received good news. Their patent had been approved.

Lamarr and Antheil were issued US Patent number 2292387. It was a 17-year patent for their Secret Communication System. But because the navy had rejected the idea, the invention was not put to use during the war. Instead, the idea was filed away.

10

ALWAYS INVENTING

Lamarr continued to star in films into the 1950s. Antheil went back to his **composing** work. All the while, their invention remained a secret. However, the government worked to develop **frequency**-hopping **technology** in the 1950s and 1960s. The navy finally put it to use in 1962. But by then, Lamarr and Antheil's patent had ended.

By 1976, the frequency hopping was called "spread **spectrum**." In the 1980s, companies began using the technology to develop electronics. Spread spectrum enabled the development of cell phones, **GPS**, and more.

Lamarr's original idea of frequency hopping was behind all of these new devices. In 1997, the Electronic Frontier Foundation honored Lamarr

DID YOU KNOW?

Different cell phones often transmit their signals on shared frequencies. Spread spectrum allows them to do this without jamming one another's signals.

with its Pioneer Award. In the following years, further honors and interviews brought Lamarr's role to light.

Lamarr lived to her mid-80s. She spent her final years in Florida, her active mind still dreaming up new tools and **technologies**. By her death on January 19, 2000, Lamarr's days in Hollywood were far behind her. But she remained an inventor to the very end.

Lamarr received a star on the Hollywood Walk of Fame for her work in film.

TIMELINE

1913 or 1914

Hedwig "Hedy" Kiesler is born on November 9 in Vienna, Austria.

1930

Hedy sneaks into a film studio near her school and is hired as an assistant.

1937

Kiesler moves to the United States and changes her last name to Lamarr.

1938

Lamarr stars in her first Hollywood film, *Algiers*.

1940

Lamarr meets composer George Antheil and tells him about her remote-controlled torpedo idea. They submit the idea to the National Inventors Council (NIC).

1942

Lamarr and Antheil receive a 17-year patent for their Secret Communication System.

1962

The US military puts Lamarr's frequency-hopping idea to use after years of development.

1980s

Commercial companies begin to use spread spectrum for consumer electronics.

HEDY LAMARR

1997

Lamarr is honored with the Electronic Frontier Foundation's Pioneer Award.

2000

Lamarr dies in her Florida home on January 19.

GLOSSARY

automatic—moving or acting by itself.

compose—to write music. A person who writes music is called a composer.

concentration camp—a camp where political prisoners are held. During World War II, many Jews were sent to concentration camps in Germany and Poland.

coordinate—to bring into a common action or movement.

engineering—the application of science and mathematics to design and create useful structures, products, or systems.

finishing school—a private school where girls from wealthy families are taught proper behavior and manners.

frequency—the number of waves, such as sound waves, passing a fixed point each second.

Global Positioning System (GPS)—a space-based navigation system used to pinpoint locations on Earth.

mechanism—a system of parts working together.

missile—a weapon that is thrown or projected to hit a target.

munitions—military equipment and supplies for fighting.

Nazi—the political party that controlled Germany under Adolf Hitler from 1933 to 1945.

random—lacking a definite plan or pattern.

scroll—a long piece of paper that rolls around one or two rods.

spectrum—an entire range of something such as light waves or radio waves.

synchronize—to cause two or more things to happen at the same time and speed.

technical—having special knowledge especially of a mechanical or scientific subject.

technology—the use of science in solving problems.

torpedo—a self-driven underwater missile shaped like a hot dog.

war bond—a certificate sold by a government to raise money for a war. The certificate promises later payment of a certain amount to the purchaser.

World War II—from 1939 to 1945, fought in Europe, Asia, and Africa. Great Britain, France, the United States, the Soviet Union, and their allies were on one side. Germany, Italy, Japan, and their allies were on the other side.

ONLINE RESOURCES

Booklinks
NONFICTION NETWORK
FREE! ONLINE NONFICTION RESOURCES

To learn more about Hedy Lamarr, visit **abdobooklinks.com**. These links are routinely monitored and updated to provide the most current information available.

INDEX